ARLINGTON COURT

Devon

Arlington Court is 7 miles north-east of Barnstaple on the A39

Acknowledgements

The catalogue of ship models was compiled by Simon Stevens of the National Maritime Museum. The section on the estate was written by Steve Mulberry, the National Trust's Property Manager, North Devon Countryside; the rest of this guide by Hugh Meller, Curator for Devon, with notes on the paintings from Alastair Laing, Adviser on Pictures and Sculpture.

Photographs: National Trust p. 34; National Trust/Bernard Kennedy-Bruyneels p. 36 (top); National Trust Photographic Library/Matthew Antrobus pp. 5, 7, 32, 33, 35, 38; NTPL/Joe Cornish p. 40; NTPL/ Jim Hallett p. 39: NTPL/John Hammond pp. 4, 9, 10, 11, 12, 14, 17, 26, 28 (top and bottom), 29, 31, 37, 48, back cover; NTPL/ Andrew Lawson p. 41; NTPL/Nadia MacKenzie front cover, pp. 1, 8, 13, 15, 16, 19, 20, 21, 22, 25 (top and bottom), 30, 36 (bottom), 42, 44, 46; Nicholas Toyne p. 27; Waverley Photographic Ltd p. 24.

First published in Great Britain in 1996 by the National Trust

Registered charity no. 205846

Reprinted with revisions 1999, 2002, 2005; revised 2004

ISBN 1-84359-048-4

Designed by James Shurmer

Phototypeset in Monotype Bembo Series 270
by Intraspan Ltd, Smallfield, Surrey (IS294)

Print managed by Astron for the National Trust (Enterprises) Ltd,
36 Queen Anne's Gate, London SW1H 9AS

CONTENTS

Introduction *page* 5

Plan of the House 6

Chapter One Tour of the House 7

Family Tree 25

Chapter Two The Chichester Family 26

Chapter Three The History of Arlington Court 32

Chapter Four The Pleasure Grounds and Estate 34

Plan of the Estate 41

Catalogue of Ship Models 42

Bibliography 48

INTRODUCTION

In a quiet corner of north Devon between Exmoor and the sea lies the thickly wooded valley of the River Yeo, and at its heart is the unassuming, but comfortable home of the Chichester family – Arlington Court.

The history of the house is as straightforward as its architecture. The main block was built in 1820 for Colonel John Chichester by a Barnstaple architect, Thomas Lee, in a severe Greek Revival style. Inside the house, the best remaining example of Lee's work is the suite of sunny rooms along the south front.

In 1865 the Colonel's grandson, Sir Bruce Chichester, enlarged the Staircase Hall, which is filled with mementoes of his passion for yacht racing. He created the formal garden and also added the servants' wing to the north, thereby completing the house as we know it.

What makes Arlington so special is not the house, but its extraordinary contents, which were largely assembled by Sir Bruce's only child, Rosalie. She was a compulsive collector with wide-ranging interests, among them her pewter and model ship collections which are exceptional by any standard. Such was the size and disparity of the collections that the National Trust was compelled to reorganise and reduce them, but it has continued the tradition set by Miss Chichester through the creation of a carriage museum in the Stables. Some 50 horse-drawn vehicles are now housed there, making it one of the finest collections in the country.

Miss Chichester was also an enthusiastic traveller, and it was as the result of one of her world tours that she was prompted by Antipodean examples to create her own wildlife park at Arlington and contemplate its gift to the National Trust, many years before the Trust had formally adopted the policy of country-house management. Accordingly, on her death in 1949, the Trust became the owner of Arlington Court and its 3,500 acres. The National Trust continues to keep a small flock of Jacob sheep and a herd of Shetland ponies – offspring of animals first kept in the park by this remarkable woman.

(Left) The Staircase Hall c.1914; watercolour by Chrissy Peters (Staircase Hall)

(Right) The main block was built in 1820, and the servants' wing (on the right) added in 1865

PLAN OF THE HOUSE

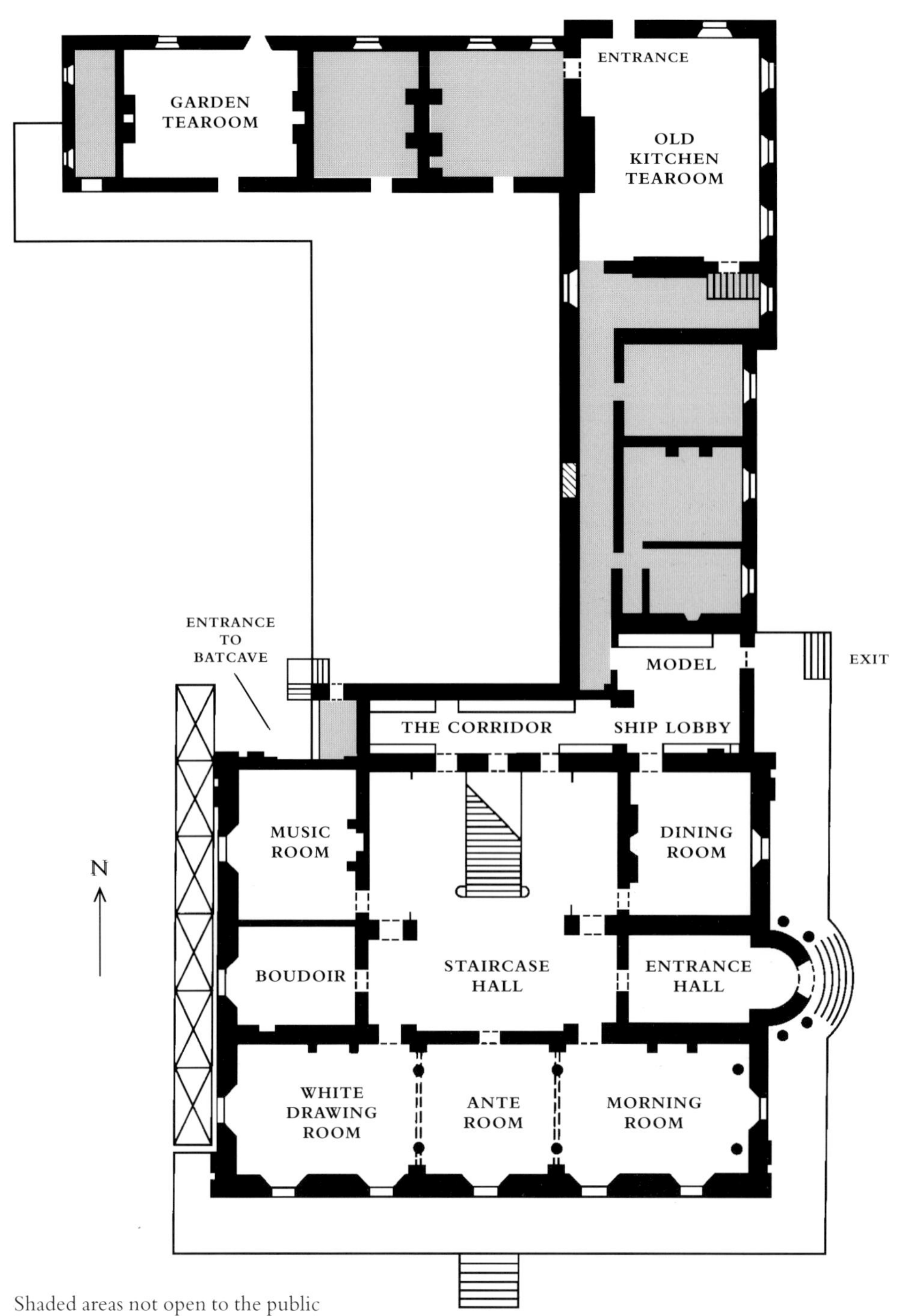

Shaded areas not open to the public

CHAPTER ONE

TOUR OF THE HOUSE

The Exterior

Miss Chichester could never bear to cut down trees, and despite necessary pruning in recent years, the house approach is still well wooded with a thick ground cover of rhododendrons and brilliant blue-flowering hydrangeas. Visitors approach the house from its north-east corner, where a long Victorian wing is easily distinguished from the grey stone Regency house that follows. Only the semicircular Doric portico and the slightest of paired Tuscan pilasters at each corner relieve this otherwise austere block.

The iron balustrade above the portico is an original feature restored by the National Trust in 1978 with a grant from the Ironmongers' Company.

The Doric portico

At basement level the stone terrace surrounding the house does not appear in the architect's original design and may have been built as an afterthought. In any event, there is an abrupt halt in its progress against the west front, alleviated since 1988 by the addition of a pergola.

The Interior

THE ENTRANCE HALL

The little hall is furnished with Chichester memorabilia evocative of a privileged Victorian family life. Portraits, election results, Court presentation photographs and yachting souvenirs are included among the more usual furnishings of a country house hall. A photograph on the north wall shows the young Miss Chichester in 1880 with her pony Czarina.

MODEL SHIP

Miss Chichester's collection of model ships is described on *p. 42.*

The visitor passes through the Staircase Hall and returns to it on several occasions during the tour, but now turns left into the Morning Room.

THE MORNING ROOM

South of the Staircase Hall are the three most important rooms in the house, now shown as one large tripartite gallery 70 feet long, punctuated by pairs of scagliola Ionic columns. In fact, by using folding screens, the gallery can be divided into three rooms, a not uncommon arrangement in early nineteenth-century houses.

This room was originally a dining-room: the two

The Morning Room

white marble-framed openings either side of the east window gave access to the food lifts that once connected with the kitchen, which was then immediately below in the basement. The room retains its original decorative plaster ceiling, together with paint and wallpaper unaltered since 1839.

In the 1860s Sir Bruce moved the dining-room to the opposite corner of the house to be nearer his new kitchen wing. This then became the Morning Room, taking advantage of the sun on the east side of the house.

WALLPAPER

Sir John Chichester had married in 1838, and correspondence in 1839 with John Crace the London decorator suggests his firm extensively redecorated Arlington for the newly married pair. Crace probably supplied the green and cream Rococo Revival wallpaper, which may be French in origin. The pattern was adjusted to fit the room, with the central six widths on the fireplace wall elaborated by adding intermediate floral motifs between the main designs.

FIREPLACE

The fireplace is of Devon Ashburton marble inserted in the 1860s.

COLLECTIONS

Everywhere there is evidence of Miss Chichester's collections: ships, shells and bibelots, displayed by her as an attractive medley impervious to museum classifications.

A Kitchen Scene; by K. K. Lauter (Morning Room)

PICTURES

MARIA PIXELL (active 1793–1811)
Old Arlington Court
Three paintings, two signed and dated 1797
The Chichesters' previous home near the church, a comfortable Georgian house with a large central bow front. It was demolished *c.*1820.

FLANKING FIREPLACE:

K. K. LAUTER (active eighteenth century)
Two Kitchen Scenes
This Tyrolean artist specialised in kitchen still-lifes.

ABOVE GLAZED CABINET:

After JAN 'VELVET' BRUEGHEL (1568–1625)
The Animals gathering to enter the Ark
The original, dated 1613, is in the Getty Museum, Malibu.

OVER DOOR:

FRANS FRANCKEN II (1581–1642)
The Worship of the Golden Calf
A stock subject with Francken, who excelled in busy figure compositions.

FURNISHINGS

AGAINST SOUTH WALL:

The ebony chest on stand inlaid with mother-of-pearl, silver, lapis lazuli and plaques of agate is an early eighteenth-century Italian piece.

The Crace wallpaper in the Morning Room

ON MANTELPIECE:

The pair of cast-brass oil lamps is unusual in having a clockwork snuffing mechanism.

LIGHTING

The cut-glass gasolier was found in the boathouse at Fell Foot, Windermere, a National Trust property, and intended for use in the eighteenth-century mansion there, which was never completed.

CARPET

A modern copy of an early nineteenth-century carpet formerly at Ashburnham Place in Sussex.

THE ANTE ROOM

Thomas Lee trained in the office of Sir John Soane, and nowhere else in the house is the great man's influence so apparent. The shallow dome, the segmental arches and the mirrored panels are pure Soane, even if the ceiling plasterwork is rather too ornate and the junction of arches and piers a little uneasy. Surviving letters in the Chichester archive dated 1839 seem to refer to this and adjoining rooms. The first, from George Trollope, concerns a shipment of furniture from London, the problem of glass breaking in transit and the employment of a grainer, perhaps the man who maple-grained the woodwork here. A second from John Crace to Sir John Chichester trusts 'that the pilasters have arrived quite safely', presumably meaning the yellow scagliola pilasters. The red silk wall-hangings also appear to be contemporary.

In Miss Chichester's day the room was screened off from the White Drawing Room and set aside for her canaries. These birds lived in an enormous brass cage set before the window. Canaries, budgerigars and a parrot were a constant element in Miss Chichester's life; their cages were placed in several rooms. The parrot was allowed to roam freely, causing havoc to the curtains, and peacocks from the garden would regularly enter via the French windows to be fed titbits.

SHOWCASES

These are full of precious things made of gold, silver, enamel, glass, jade and rock crystal. Most were acquired by Miss Chichester. Of local interest are the pair of seventeenth-century silver mugs by

The Arlington Court Picture; by William Blake, 1821 (Ante Room)

John Peard the Younger and the sixteenth-century silver spoons made in Barnstaple.

PICTURES

WILLIAM BLAKE (1757–1827)
The Arlington Court Picture
Signed: *W Blake Inventor 1821*
Ink, watercolour and bodycolour over a gesso ground on paper
The painting's date and the fact that – quite exceptionally – it is in its original frame (by James Linnell), suggest that it was probably brought to Arlington by Colonel John Chichester before his death in 1823. It was found by National Trust staff in 1949 on top of a pantry cupboard. Nothing is known of whom it was painted for, and none of Blake's voluminous writings refers to it. It has been explained by Kathleen Raine as an allegory inspired by a neo-Platonic interpretation of the *Odyssey*, but this, like other purported explications of it, is entirely arbitrary. The unique form of Blake's signature underlines the personal nature of its symbolism, to which we lack the key.

GEORGE BICKHAM (1684–1769) after
WILLIAM AIKMAN (1682–1731)
John Gay (1685–1732)
Engraving, published 1729
The author of *The Beggar's Opera*, who was born in Barnstaple.

The White Drawing Room and Ante Room c.1914; by Chrissy Peters

The curious portraits of two girls made from strips of paper were designed to be viewed from an angle and are known as an anamorphic projection.

SCULPTURE

ON WINDOW SILL:

The marble effigy commemorates Sir Bruce Chichester's dog Memory.

THE WHITE DRAWING ROOM

Miss Chichester spent much of her time here, accompanied by her parrot Polly, who was allowed to fly freely in this sunny room.

The ceiling plasterwork is original, mirroring that in the Morning Room, but, by contrast, the wallpaper has been changed at regular intervals, most recently in 1984, when the whole room was redecorated by the National Trust.

PICTURES

LEFT OF MANTELPIECE, ABOVE:

Caroline Thistlethwayte
Miss Chichester's paternal grandmother.

RIGHT OF MANTELPIECE, ABOVE:

Amelia Onslow
Miss Chichester's maternal grandmother.

OVER DOORS:

By, and in the manner of, FRANS FRANCKEN II (1581–1642) and Studio
The Triumph of Neptune and Amphitrite
Two paintings on copper
Amphitrite, Neptune's initially reluctant bride, is carried over the waves on dolphins' backs.

OPPOSITE:

Baron von KLANK, 1870, after a follower of LORENZO DI CREDI (*c.*1458–1537)
Madonna and Child and two Angels
Given by Miss Jelley, a friend of Miss Chichester's, in 1973.

FURNISHINGS

The room contains some unusual souvenirs Miss Chichester collected on her travels, most notably the Chinese red amber elephant and the Pacific Island conch shell. More conventional is the collection of English and French snuff boxes and oriental jade pieces in the glazed cabinet against the south wall and on the glass-topped table beside the settee.

Miss Chichester's writing-table is contemporary with the house. This handsome walnut and yew-wood piece with dolphin-shaped supporting brackets is a pair to one in the west window, by a Barnstaple cabinetmaker.

The two card-tables were also locally made in the early nineteenth century.

The gilt chairs are all that is left of a suite of similar furniture that once filled this room.

IN FAR LEFT CORNER OF ROOM:

A thirteenth-century Flemish psalter with historiated initials. In the early seventeenth century it was owned by Robert Hill, a London divine, but how it came to Arlington is not known.

CARPET

A hand-knotted Donegal made in 1978 as a replica of one that had been in the room since the 1820s. In the centre is the Chichester monogram and in each corner the family crest of a heron with an eel in its bill.

LIGHTING

The chandelier is also probably Irish, made of Waterford glass in the late eighteenth century.

The visitor leaves the room, goes into the Staircase Hall and turns left into the Boudoir.

THE BOUDOIR

The Boudoir balances the Entrance Hall opposite. It is a charming little room, intended as a ladies' retreat, a character it still retains. Doubtless it is part of Lee's original design, distinguished by the plaster ceiling with rosettes framed in mouldings of acanthus leaves, and the faded rose and gold silk wall-hangings. During the latter part of the nineteenth century the Italianate pilasters either side of the mirrored corners and the enamel splays in the Ashburton marble fireplace were added.

PICTURES

OVER CHIMNEYPIECE:

Sir GEORGE CHALMERS, Bt (1720–91)
Elizabeth and Mary Chichester
Painted in 1777

The Boudoir

The sisters of the builder of the house, aged five and nine, with their pet lamb and a basket of doves. They were the daughters of Mary MacDonald and John Chichester. Chalmers was a Jacobite heraldic artist who learnt portraiture and practised in Hull *c.*1777–81, when he would have painted this and the portrait of their mother (Dining Room) at Burton Constable in Yorkshire.

RIGHT OF MANTELPIECE:

Colonel John Chichester (1769–1823)
A silhouette of the builder of the house.

FURNITURE AND CERAMICS

AGAINST RIGHT-HAND WALL:

A large eighteenth-century English secretaire bookcase in satinwood inlaid with kingwood, ebony and holly. It contains a tea service in Chinese porcelain of the Quianlong period, *c.*1790, painted with the arms of Colonel Chichester.

The small chairs and tables painted and decorated with mother-of-pearl are made of papier mâché.

Bruce and Caroline Chichester; by J. E. Williams, 1849 (Music Room)

RIGHT OF DOOR:

The English looking-glass of the 1690s retains its original glass, framed by panels of seaweed marquetry in walnut and holly.

Returning to the Staircase Hall and turning left, go through the next door into the Music Room.

THE MUSIC ROOM

When the National Trust acquired Arlington in 1949, the room was suffering from wood rot at a time when staff flats were needed on the upper floor. Government restrictions on building work after the war meant that only the second task could be tackled, and the room regrettably was not restored. The painted ceiling depicting musical motifs and the papier-mâché fillet round the walls were lost.

In 1998 the room was redecorated to represent the room as it was before 1949 but the lack of any visual or documentary records means this cannot be exact.

PICTURES

ON LEFT-HAND WALL:

JOHN EDGAR WILLIAMS (active 1846–83)
Bruce and Caroline Chichester as children
Signed and dated 1849
Sir Bruce Chichester as a boy, seated on a donkey held by his sister Caroline, later Lady Clay. Both children are wearing Maltese costume; Caroline's dress survives and stands nearby in the glass case.

OVER FIREPLACE:

After RUBENS
The Rape of Proserpine
Painted on copper

FURNITURE AND CERAMICS

ON OPPOSITE WALL:

The huge oak bookcase is original to the house. It is filled with ceramics, notably oriental, Meissen and Sèvres pieces. One shelf supports a collection of pots presented to Miss Chichester by Sir Leonard Woolley in gratitude for her help in funding his archaeological expedition to the ancient city of Ur, now in Iraq.

The grand piano by A.-J. Bord of Paris was built in 1886 and is the only example by that maker in the National Trust's possession.

The model ships are described on p.42.

Return to the Staircase Hall.

THE STAIRCASE HALL

Because of the abundance of yachting pictures and the flamboyant Victorian imperial staircase, this room has often been compared to a yacht club. Justly so, as the man who created it, Sir Bruce Chichester, was a keen sailor and a lavish spender.

In 1865 Sir Bruce demolished the old staircase in the north-west corner of the Hall and built the present one in the space created by absorbing two rooms each on the ground and first floors into his new hall. The stairs now ascend, guarded by a pair of yacht's cannon, to a landing lit by three windows, each containing stained glass.

STAINED GLASS

The heraldic shields commemorate Chichester marriages from 1505 to Sir Bruce's own in 1865.

LIGHTING

The lantern above, *c.*1810, came from Buckland House at Braunton.

An heraldic shield to commemorate the marriage of Sir John Chichester of Ralegh to Margaret Beaumont in 1505

The Staircase Hall

PICTURES

ABOVE DOOR TO BOUDOIR:

Erminia
Five watercolours and two oil paintings depicting the topsail schooner purchased by Sir Bruce in 1869. It was in this boat at the age of three that his daughter Rosalie travelled to the Mediterranean and acquired her taste for ships. There are two more paintings of the yacht in contemporary rope-bordered frames on the south wall.

RIGHT OF BOUDOIR DOOR:

CHRISSY PETERS (d.1939)
Six interior views of Arlington
Six watercolours by Miss Chichester's long-time companion, which show interiors of the house as it was in 1914. The hall is depicted filled with books, pictures, flowers, stuffed animals and birds, and large glass cases containing model boats.

BENEATH GALLERY OPPOSITE:

WILLIAM DREDGE (active 1840–60)
The intended Suspension Bridge at Arlington Court
Signed and dated 1849
A sketch of the bridge Sir John Chichester planned to cross the lake he had created in the park. Dredge was an engineer who had previously designed two bridges for friends of the Chichesters in Ireland. The piers were indeed built as shown, but on Sir John's death in 1851 the bridge, which would have had a main span of 200 feet, was unfinished and the project never completed.

A watercolour by Miss Chichester of her beloved parrot Polly, which was allowed to fly freely around the house

JAMES HOWELL (1786–1866)
Unexecuted design for new service wings at Arlington Court
Signed and dated 1849
Howell was president of the Surveyors' Club and had designed Southwick Park, Hampshire, for Sir John's father-in-law.

THOMAS LEE (1794–1834)
Arlington Court
A perspective drawing of Lee's Arlington, dated 1822, when it was exhibited at the Royal Academy.

BELOW LANDING:

WILLIAM HOARE of Bath, RA (1707–92)
Grecian women, a pair
Related to similar compositions drawn in pastel at Stourhead in Wiltshire, and elsewhere – nudities purporting to be representations of the seasons.

FURNISHINGS

Apart from the ship models, the Hall contains part of Miss Chichester's enormous collection of shells, an impressive scrap-screen dating from the early nineteenth century, a Collard & Collard grand piano in rosewood veneer, dated 1870, and three swords used by members of the family.

Climb the stairs and turn right into the Gallery.

THE GALLERY AND STAIRCASE

This comprises the half-landing and top gallery of Sir Bruce's new staircase, built in 1865.

FURNISHINGS

The resemblance to a yacht club is emphasised at the first landing by the ship's clock from the *Erminia*, mounted as a mantelclock, and everywhere one looks there are model ships displayed in their cases.

PICTURES

ON STAIRCASE WALLS:

Neapolitan scenes by Giuseppe Scoppa, Camillo da Vito, Mr Manton and others, souvenirs of Sir Bruce's Mediterranean voyages.

ON GALLERY WALLS:

The careful flower paintings are by Miss Peters, Miss Chichester's companion.

ON LANDING SPANDREL:

A watercolour by Miss Chichester of her parrot Polly, aged 40. Polly died in 1919, after living at Arlington for 46 years, and is buried beneath a granite slab between the rhododendron clumps in front of the house.

Turn left into the Tapestry Room.

THE TAPESTRY ROOM

This room has had various uses, particularly as a bedroom, usually reserved for guests, and as a box room. It was previously known as the Blue Room having once been decorated in blue.

It now houses the four 18th century Beauvais tapestries which were probably acquired for Arlington by John Palmer Chichester in 1796. The tapestries used to hang in the Museum Room on the north-west flank of the house but this was demolished in 1950. They were woven in silk and wool and are in excellent condition having always been protected from direct sunlight.

Each tapestry illustrates one of four continents with added symbolism reflecting French ambitions at the time. America depicts Minerva, Goddess of War, threatening the overthrown British power symbolised by Britannia. A bust of Washington is fixed to a column signifying American independence. Europe portrays Minerva presiding over the independent states symbolised by their escutcheons. The fruits of peace are evident whilst the Horse of War makes off to the right. Africa is more exotic in colour and subject-matter including a large cotton tree and an obelisk from Ancient Egypt, a country then being explored. A European woman proffers riches to the African ruler. Asia is richer still in colour and is intended to demonstrate the wealth of variety found in the continent. Unlike earlier versions of the subject, the Beauvais set also includes references to China.

THE PORTICO ROOM

The room sits above the Entrance Hall and has a curious vaulted ceiling. In 1980 it was refurnished as a sitting-room, but in the nineteenth century it was Sir John's and then Sir Bruce's bedroom.

PICTURES AND FURNITURE

Amongst the wealth of Chichester family memorabilia left to the National Trust by Miss Chichester was a large number of photograph albums. A selection of the photographs has been copied and framed. In particular, on the desk is a characteristic picture of Miss Chichester, the indomitable traveller, on her first round-the-world tour, at Rotorua, New Zealand, in 1921, accompanied by the diminutive Miss Peters (illustrated on p.31). The Victorian enthusiasm for celebrating death is also well represented by the two memorial photographic portraits of a member of the Chamberlayne (her mother's) family and Sir Bruce Chichester, both surrounded by feathers within ebonised Oxford frames.

MISS CHICHESTER'S BEDROOM

On 29 November 1865 Miss Chichester was born in this room, which was her mother's bedroom (then known as the White Room). It became her own bedroom after her mother died in 1908.

FURNITURE

The room is furnished much as Miss Chichester had it, with a large half-tester bed and many of her personal possessions.

ON CHEST OF DRAWERS:

The oak reading stand was carved by Miss Chichester herself, incorporating a dragon and her initials. Her own photographic portrait as a young woman stands in a daffodil-decorated frame next to it.

The washstand, bowl and ewer are a reminder that within living memory hot water for washing still had to be carried up by a housemaid from the kitchen.

PICTURES

More photographs copied from the family albums are on display, including three of Arlington and the church, on the fireplace wall, and a magnificent wedding picture of 1903 in the south-east corner. This shows the wedding of Miss Chichester's nephew, George Johnstone, to Lord Brownlow's daughter. To the left of this photograph is a watercolour of Miss Chichester's mother's home, Cranbury Park in Hampshire.

Miss Chichester's Bedroom

The Day Nursery

IN FIREPLACE:

ROSALIE CHICHESTER (1865–1949)
A black grouse and setter
Painted when she was seventeen.

THE DAY NURSERY

The original nursery was on the north-west side of the house, and this room, formerly Miss Chichester's dressing-room, has been fitted out by the National Trust with furniture and toys found at Arlington.

FURNITURE

The mahogany and wicker cradle was bought for Miss Chichester by her mother in the 1860s.

Among the many Victorian toys are several curiosities: the trapeze artist in the glass case; the robin and blue tit modelled in bread; the battered clockwork tortoise; and a seemingly unbreakable cast-iron walking elephant patented in 1873.

The meticulously turned ivories are by Miss Chichester's uncle, Tankerville Chamberlayne.

ON MANTELPIECE:

Two of Miss Chichester's pet mice, Mina and Mineril, stuffed and mounted under glass cases. She was an animal lover from an early age.

(Right) Some of Miss Chichester's fans, parasols and other personal possessions are displayed in the Lobby

THE LOBBY

Jan Newman worked at Arlington as a house parlourman from 1927 until his retirement in 1974. When Miss Chichester died in 1949, he helped to reorganise the house for opening by the National Trust and the arrangement of these two cabinets is his work. They are full of fans, parasols, jewellery, trinkets and family souvenirs.

Miss Chichester's own achievements are marked by the Primrose League badges she earned whilst she was the secretary of the local branch; a silver plaque awarded to her by *The Practical Photographer*; and a silver medal won in the 'Womanhood Competition'.

ON WALLS:

Three framed ensembles, each with six exotic birds executed in feathers and gouache by Lady Rosamund Christie, a cousin and neighbour of Miss Chichester, who lived at Tapeley Park in north Devon.

The Lobby leads back to the Gallery, where there are more flower paintings by Miss Chichester and Miss Peters and paintings of Sir Bruce Chichester's yacht *Zoe*. In the second of these on the right, the battleship HMS *Warrior* appears in the background, the most formidable warship in the world in the 1860s.

THE PINK BEDROOM

This room was restored in 2004. It has always been a bedroom and was for a while used by Lady Chichester after her marriage to Sir Arthur in 1883. It was originally filled with Italian furniture, brought over from Youlston House. This was sold in 1908, after Lady Chichester's death, by Miss Chichester, who disliked it. The present furnishings have been brought in from elsewhere in the house.

THE DINING ROOM

Originally the library, this room was made into a dining-room by Miss Chichester, when she converted her father's dining-room into a museum for her collections (see p. 30).

CHIMNEYPIECE

The white marble chimneypiece was salvaged from the former house in 1820. The handsome grate came from the old Reading Room, near the church.

WALLPAPER

The room was redecorated in 1995 using a wallpaper based on a nineteenth-century design by John Crace.

PICTURES

OVER CHIMNEYPIECE:

Sir GEORGE CHALMERS, Bt (1720–91)
Mary MacDonald (1737/8–1815), *Mrs Chichester*
Signed and dated 1780
The mother of Colonel John Chichester. Her father, Major Donald MacDonald of Terndreich, joined the Young Pretender in 1745, was taken prisoner after the Battle of Falkirk and hanged at Carlisle. His house was burnt by the Hanoverian troops, and Mary, aged seven, escaped and wandered forlornly about the hills for three weeks, pursued by the Duke of Cumberland's bloodhounds. Eventually, she escaped the Butcher of Culloden and arrived at the house of her kinswoman, Lady Dundonald, who brought her up and with whom she lived until she married John Chichester in 1765.

RIGHT OF FIREPLACE:

Circle of JOHN BOGLE (*c*.1746–1804)
Col John Chichester (1769–1823)
Watercolour miniature on ivory
Miss Chichester's great grandfather.

The Dining Room table set for tea

School of Richard Cosway (1742–1821)
An unknown lady, possibly Mrs Fitzherbert
Watercolour miniature

LEFT OF FIREPLACE:

Italian
Sir John Palmer Chichester (1794–1851)
Watercolour miniature on ivory
Painted in Rome in September 1835.

Emma Kendrick (1788–1851)
An unknown lady
Watercolour miniature on ivory

Other portraits in the room include:

A tinted photograph of Miss Chichester at the age of about thirteen, dressed in mourning.

Two photographs of Sir Bruce Chichester.

Sir John Chichester (1598–1669)
A Cornish MP who was knighted by Charles I.

Robert Edward Chichester (1872–1958)
Miss Chichester's stepfather's grandson.

FURNITURE

The mid-nineteenth-century mahogany sideboard and dining-table have both been introduced into the house by the National Trust. On the sideboard stand a glass wine-cooler and three menus, written in French by Miss Chichester. The table is laid with a tea service used by her. Most of the silver plate pieces are gifts from members of the Chichester family.

THE CORRIDOR

PEWTER

On the right-hand side is a collection of approximately 400 pieces of pewter, the largest and most varied of any held by the National Trust and one of the finest collections on public view outside the major museums. A few pieces bear the arms of the Chichester family, but most were acquired by Miss Chichester.

The collection's strength is in pewterware from the British Isles, but there are a few continental items including a set of three sixteenth-century flagons found at Elunberg Castle in Bavaria and two rare elaborately cast-decorated French dishes dating from the late sixteenth century. The English pewterware includes numerous seventeenth- and eighteenth-century plates, dishes and chargers up to 20½in in diameter. Notable are three fine seventeenth-century English flagons and four very rare Stuart period candlesticks. The earliest English pieces include a number of sixteenth-century spoons and an Elizabethan porringer with two clover-leaf ears. There are also baluster-shaped wine measures such as were used in taverns during the seventeenth and eighteenth centuries, a range of seventeenth- and eighteenth-century salts, a large collection of snuff boxes, including a pair in the shape of duelling pistols, and several inkwells.

Scottish pewterware is well represented by long sets of ale and spirit measures. The earliest is a pot-bellied measure from the late seventeenth century. There are several tappit hen measures of the early nineteenth century, but the most interesting is a possibly unique set of mid-nineteenth-century thistle-shaped measures. They are rare, because soon after they were issued it was discovered that they did not drain fully and should have been destroyed; very few escaped. Also Scottish are the snuff mills mounted on animal hoofs and horns, and a few inscribed pieces from Scottish churches.

Irish pewter is represented by two half-pint handleless baluster measures and a set of 'hay stack' measures, the largest of these being an impressive one of a gallon capacity. There are also nine tall, lidded eighteenth-century measures from the Channel Islands in a range of sizes and styles typical of both Jersey and Guernsey.

Miscellaneous items include tobacco boxes, tea caddies, a processional mace, a bottle drainer, ornate ship models and spoons in both pewter and latten (an early form of brass). Among the pewter spoons are several with a cast portrait of Queen Anne at the end of the stem. These were made as coronation souvenirs in 1702.

SHELLS

EITHER SIDE OF THE PEWTER:

The shells are partly Miss Chichester's collection, including four precious Golden Cowries, and partly Mr T. F. Higham's gift of conchological decorative art at its most elaborate.

CERAMICS

Miss Chichester's collection of Royal Commemorative pottery mugs and plates dates from Queen Victoria's Golden Jubilee of 1887 onwards. Included is a double-handle mug made in advance for the abortive coronation of King Edward VIII. More recently the National Trust's own commemorative mugs have been added to the collection.

MISCELLANEA

AT END OF CORRIDOR:

A bell, engraved 'Maria', probably French of fifteenth-century date, which used to hang in a small belfry above the service wing at Arlington and tolled to regulate working hours on the estate.

ABOVE:

The family's pedigree, drawn on vellum.

ON THE SOUTH WALL:

The bird and *still life* studies are by Miss Chichester.

Return down the Corridor and enter the Ship Lobby.

THE SHIP LOBBY

SHIP MODELS

The remainder of Miss Chichester's collection of ship models is displayed here, including twelve of the immortal 'Little Ships' which rescued the British Army from the beaches of Dunkirk in 1940. Miss Chichester had these made just after the war to recall the defeat which turned into victory. (See p.42 for a full list.)

Here too the National Trust has placed a specially commissioned model of *Gypsy Moth IV*, in which Sir Francis Chichester completed his epic solo world voyage in 1967. Sir Francis's father was Rector of Shirwell, the parish next to Arlington, and the young Francis Chichester was a frequent visitor to his aunt and the woods at Arlington.

PICTURES

LEFT OF GARDEN DOOR:

ROSALIE CHICHESTER
Watercolour of Arlington Lake, 1880

The Kitchen in use around 1900

W. WHATMAN
Watercolour of Arlington Court, 1845

DENZIL REEVES
Watercolour, Arlington capriccio, 1987

RIGHT OF GARDEN DOOR:

FANNY CHICHESTER (b.1838)
View of Appledore from Instow

ROSALIE CHICHESTER
Watercolour of a boat

Leave by the garden door. To the left is the Old Kitchen Tearoom.

THE OLD KITCHEN

This room began life as a kitchen. Photographs now hung on the walls, copied from the family albums, show it in use at the turn of the century. The 1871 census provides a glimpse of domestic life at Arlington by listing all the staff resident on the night of 2 April. They were: Mary Hall the housekeeper, two lady's maids (for the five-year-old Rosalie's mother and grandmother), Sarah Butt (Rosalie's 48-year-old nanny), a head housemaid, three other maids, Alfred Morse the butler, a young footman, two grooms and a sixteen-year-old lad. This totals thirteen and does not include Sir Bruce's man-servant, or the estate and gardening staff. In the 1920s there were still seven indoor staff at Arlington, but after 1945 only two.

FIREPLACE

The stone fireplace was brought from the Museum Room, when it was demolished in 1949. It stands in place of the iron cooking range.

THE KITCHEN AND TEA-ROOM

The present kitchen was Sir Bruce Chichester's workshop. The tea-room beyond was originally the servants' hall, with the butler's quarters on the first floor above it.

THE CHICHESTERS OF ARLINGTON

These stained-glass coats of arms in the Staircase Hall commemorate the marriages of Sir John Chichester of Ralegh to Margaret Beaumont in 1505 (above) and John Chichester of Arlington to Mary MacDonald in 1764 (below)

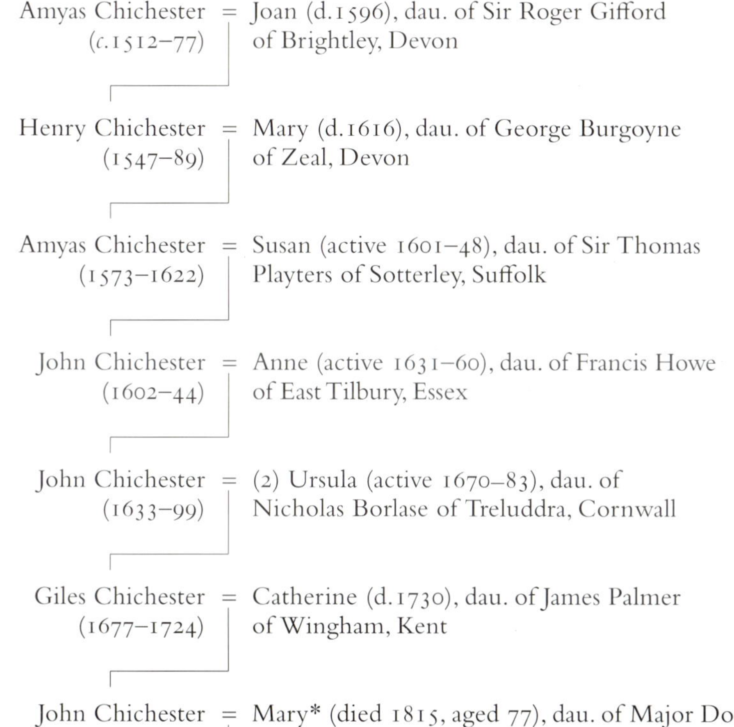

Amyas Chichester (*c.*1512–77) = Joan (d.1596), dau. of Sir Roger Gifford of Brightley, Devon

Henry Chichester (1547–89) = Mary (d.1616), dau. of George Burgoyne of Zeal, Devon

Amyas Chichester (1573–1622) = Susan (active 1601–48), dau. of Sir Thomas Playters of Sotterley, Suffolk

John Chichester (1602–44) = Anne (active 1631–60), dau. of Francis Howe of East Tilbury, Essex

John Chichester (1633–99) = (2) Ursula (active 1670–83), dau. of Nicholas Borlase of Treluddra, Cornwall

Giles Chichester (1677–1724) = Catherine (d.1730), dau. of James Palmer of Wingham, Kent

John Chichester (1707–83) = Mary* (died 1815, aged 77), dau. of Major Donald MacDonald of Terndreich, Inverness

Colonel John Chichester* (1769–1823) builder of Arlington Court = (2) Agnes (d.1814), dau. of James Hamilton of Bangour, Linlithgowshire | Mary* | Elizabeth*

Sir John Chichester* cr. Bt 1840 (1794–1851) = Caroline*, dau. of Thomas Thistlethwayte of Southwick Park, Hampshire

Sir Bruce Chichester* 2nd Bt (1842–81) = Rosalie (d.1908), dau. of Thomas Chamberlayne of Cranbury Park, Hampshire m.1865 | Caroline Lady Clay* (1839–73)

Rosalie Chichester* (1865–1949) d.s.p.

* denotes a portrait in the house

CHAPTER TWO

THE CHICHESTER FAMILY

Arlington as we see it today was created by the last four generations of the Chichesters, but they came from an ancient family which had settled in north Devon around 1385, when John Chichester married the heiress Thomasine Ralegh.

The Raleghs were an even older family than the Chichesters and had lived in north Devon since before the Conquest; indeed a Ralegh was allegedly killed at the battle of Hastings. Thomasine, who lies buried in Arlington church, bore a son, John, who is said to have fought at Agincourt. His great-great-grandson, Amyas, was born in about 1512 and was bequeathed the Arlington property in his father's will, thereby establishing the Arlington branch of the Chichester family. In *The Worthies of Devon* (1701), John Prince described 'the strange fertility of that branch thereof which yet flourisheth at Arlington':

> Amias Chichester of that place, Esquire, by Joan his wife ... had 19 sons; every one of which (what you may think much stranger) had no less than four sisters; 14 of the 19 lived to be proper gentlemen; though not above 3 of them had issue. When they went all to church the first would be in the church porch before the last would be out of the house.

This story is recalled by Charles Kingsley in his novel *Westward Ho!* (1855).

Amyas's son Henry succeeded his father in 1577 and set the family on a course it was to follow for over 200 years by remaining a practising Roman

St James's church and Old Arlington Court, which was built by Colonel Chichester around 1790 and demolished only 30 years later; by Maria Pixell (Morning Room)

Catholic after the Reformation. Like other Catholic families, the Chichesters actively supported the Royalist cause during the Civil War. In a report to Parliament in 1642 it was said, 'There hath been more substantial armour found at Mr Chichester's house at Arlington and Master Courtenay his house at Molland, than in our whole county.'

The family was heavily penalised financially for its faith, but prosperity returned when Giles, the eldest son of the next generation, married Catherine Palmer, the niece and heiress of the Earl of Castlemaine, who inherited considerable estates in Wales. Their son John married Mary MacDonald, whose father, Major Donald MacDonald, had joined the Young Pretender in 1745. He had been captured after the battle of Falkirk and hanged at Carlisle (see p. 21).

The next in line was another John, usually known as Colonel Chichester, a rank he achieved in commanding the Cardiganshire Militia. At Arlington he left his mark by building two houses, the first so badly that it survived only 30 years; the second is the present house, which was completed in the year of his death, 1823. In 1793 Colonel Chichester married as his second wife Agnes Hamilton, a Protestant, and as a result also became a Protestant. In his *Collections Illustrating the History of the Catholic Families in Devon and Cornwall*, Dr Oliver lamented:

> The Chichesters of Arlington persevered in the religion of their forefathers, until the representative of this ancient family, John Palmer Chichester, read his incantation in Exeter Cathedral in 1793. Until this unhappy defection, a priest had been maintained as chaplain in the family. But after this event, the oldest chaplaincy in Devon was closed up, and the last incumbent, the Reverend Henry Innes, was turned adrift.

John Palmer Bruce Chichester succeeded his father after an active naval career. For ten years, 1831–41, he represented Barnstaple in Parliament and was created a baronet in 1840. To him is due the planting of much of the woodland round the park and the creation of the lake in the valley below (see p. 39). When he died in 1851, his son, Sir Bruce Chichester, the last of the male line, was still a minor. Once he attained his majority in 1863, Arlington enjoyed a typically golden Victorian era. He spent lavishly on building projects and entertainments, as befitted a country gentleman who was a magistrate, a captain in the North Devon Yeomanry and High Sheriff of Devon in 1868. The house was doubled in size by the addition of an enlarged staircase hall and a new service wing and dining-room; smart new stables followed. Dances,

(Right) Sir Bruce Chichester in his uniform as a captain in the North Devon Yeomanry

Sir Bruce's schooner 'Erminia', painted in 1869 (Staircase Hall)

garden parties, flower shows, hunting and cricket matches were a regular part of the social round, Sir Bruce himself frequently playing in the Arlington Eleven.

His other great extravagance was yacht racing. In 1865 he had married Rosalie, the daughter of Thomas Chamberlayne, a keen yachtsman, whose cutter *Arrow* was the most famous of all mid-nineteenth-century racing yachts and the only British yacht to defeat the schooner *America* (after which the America's Cup is named). Sir Bruce was a member of the Royal Yacht Squadron and owned the schooners *Zoe* and *Erminia*, the latter a vast boat of 276 tons. As a child of three and again as a girl of twelve, Sir Bruce's only child, Rosalie Caroline, was taken on long Mediterranean cruises in the *Erminia*.

On the second cruise, in 1877, Rosalie kept a diary, still preserved at Arlington, which recounts how she took photographs, learned to row, had drawing lessons from a Professor Lanza at Naples, acquired a monkey at Gibraltar and survived a number of storms. The worst of these makes graphic reading:

Friday 21st December 1877. Last night about 12 o'clock I woke hearing the sailors reefing the mainsail and taking the gib down. A lot of calling and the wind roaring and whistling. Then my soap dish cover gave a

Rosalie Chichester with her mother around 1870

The Morning Room c.1914; watercolour by Chrissy Peters

jump and fell breaking to the ground, for the ship was jumping. My bed – a swinging one – was screwed up. Papa came in and asked if I would like it undone, but I did not. I then rolled from side to side and up and down again. It was good fun. My chair took a walk across my room. After a time it fell over, all my clothes on it fell about. I had to call Smith to undo my bed, then it swung so far that I could not go farther. I jumped out of bed to peep in the main cabin; I never saw anything like it, the books were all over the ground, a chair tumbled over. After a little, fell asleep. Woke up and saw my toilet cover off the chest of drawers, books, work etc. strewn about. No-one could stand. Got on deck, but dared not move.

For Miss Chichester these experiences of the sea later inspired her to travel all over the world and to make her own vast collection of model ships and shells, but sadly it was on this voyage that her father contracted 'Maltese fever', from which he never fully recovered. He died three years later, in 1881, leaving his estate heavily mortgaged.

It took his widow and daughter nearly 50 years to pay all the debts. The house staff was cut by half, land was sold and efforts made to develop the Chichester property at Woolacombe into 'one of the most attractive seaside resorts in the West'; as the local press reported, 'One important feature of this work is that nothing of the seaboard will be destroyed and all the natural features of the locality will be retained', but the scheme came to nothing for lack of cash. In 1883 Lady Chichester married Sir Arthur Chichester, a distant cousin of her first husband who lived at Youlston some five miles away, and Rosalie Chichester took over the task of running the Arlington estate where she was to spend the rest of her long life. In 1885 she was presented at Court 'among the many debutantes who were much noticed and whose toilets were especially elegant . . . dressed very simply in white broché and tulle wearing a garniture of natural marguerites and fern'. But she never married: the indebted state of her inheritance may have put off potential suitors. Being far from London and without friends or family in the capital, she was obliged to find her own occupations locally as best she could, and this she did with tremendous energy.

Rosalie Chichester observed the landowner's traditional duties in providing entertainments and activities for her tenants and villagers and especially the local schoolchildren. She also became interested in politics. With her mother, she founded a local branch of the Primrose League after Disraeli's death in 1881, and was not averse to giving 'a spirited address' to League members in north Devon over a period of some ten years. For a while she wrote a monthly newspaper, *The Arlington Review*, packed with information and comment on national and international affairs. She seems to have received little formal education, and the newspaper may have been an attempt to put this right. It also reveals her wide-ranging interests, politics and traditional values. She wrote regularly for the *Daily Sketch*, and produced several unpublished novels that she scribbled into notebooks. These are romantic rambles, but in them Miss Chichester's sympathies clearly lie with the paternalistic notion of aristocratic leadership centred around the family seat. Later in life she participated in local organisations such as the War Agricultural Committee, the Women's Land Army and the Women's Citizenship Association.

Miss Chichester's silver-mounted dressing-table set in her bedroom

Miss Chichester was also always interested and knowledgeable in scientific and practical matters. She invented gadgets which she had patented, but did little to modernise the running of the house (mains electricity was not introduced until 1951). She was an astronomer who built her own observatory in the garden, she was a keen photographer, winning prizes for her pictures which she developed and printed herself; and she painted, especially local landscapes, flowers and animals; but above all she collected.

Today only a fraction of Rosalie Chichester's collections are shown in the house, as her collector's instinct became a mania. By the time the National Trust inherited Arlington in 1949, she had amassed 75 cabinets full of shells, 200 model ships, several hundred pieces of pewter, 50 punch ladles, 30 tea caddies, two cases full of candle snuffers, two cases of Maori skirts and African clubs, five large cases of stuffed birds, hundreds of snuff boxes, a large stamp collection with some 52,000 specimens, 30 volumes of Christmas and greeting cards, and others containing photographs, feathers, family crests, letter heads and other ephemera, 40 paperweights, 29 watches, numerous mineral specimens, medals, coins, books (including five sixteenth-century books unknown to bibliographers), brass and glass objects, a cupboard full of camera equipment and 'a case of bombs and zeppelin bits'.

The National Trust was forced to sell some of these treasures and pass some to its other houses. It is easy now to criticise this action, but it should be remembered that stringent government economies controlled development plans at that time, and the National Trust lacked much of the expertise it enjoys today. There was also a practical reason for the dispersal, since only then could visitors safely tour the house, which would otherwise have been far too crowded.

Jan Newman, who worked at Arlington for 47 years, has recorded his first impression of the Staircase Hall in 1927:

Miss Chichester (centre right) and her companion Chrissy Peters (centre left) in New Zealand during their 1921 tour

The hall enthralled me with its great cases of stuffed birds, butterflies, an albatross, a kangaroo and a large bear; while on top of the cabinets were sets of *famille rose* china, great dishes and vases decorated with animals and insects.

Although Miss Chichester's quiet life gave her the time to collect on this scale, she was not a recluse. Her tea parties were well-known, and among her friends was Canon Rawnsley, one of the three founders of the National Trust in 1895. In 1908 her mother died and Miss Chichester gave the first of several gifts of land on the north Devon coast to the National Trust in memory of her parents.

In 1912 Miss Chichester was joined at Arlington by Miss Chrissy Peters, as a paid companion. She too was a practical person, whose abilities proved useful at Arlington. Single-handed, she wired up a system of bells connecting the reception rooms to the servants' corridor and made two crystal wireless sets – one of them for the servants' hall. She was also an able artist, whose watercolour sketches of Arlington have become a valuable record, and a keen traveller, accompanying Miss Chichester on two world tours. In 1921 the pair visited Australia and New Zealand, where Miss Chichester was much impressed by the National Parks. At Arlington she began opening the grounds to visitors during the summer months (as many as 300 a day would travel from Ilfracombe by charabanc) and she approached the National Trust as early as 1921 about the future of Arlington, long before the Trust's country-house scheme was first mooted.

In 1939 Miss Peters died and the combination of wartime restrictions and increasing ill health meant that Miss Chichester's last years were lonely and painful. Nancy Phelan paid a visit during the war:

The morning-room was smallish and darkish and crammed with furniture – footstools, what-nots, *gueridons*, easels, cabinets full of knicknacks. There was an impression of thick plush curtains and velvet upholstery, of fringes and screens. Enthroned amongst the clutter, in a black shapeless garment, was Miss Chichester.

On her death in 1949 she completed her gift to the National Trust not only of Arlington Court, but also of the entire estate.

CHAPTER THREE

THE HISTORY OF ARLINGTON COURT

The present Arlington Court is the third, or perhaps fourth, house built by the Chichester family near the church of St James. Tradition has it that a manor house stood south of the church, at least from the sixteenth century. This was demolished in about 1790 by Colonel Chichester, who employed a London architect and surveyor, John Meadows (*c.*1732–91), to build a new house on the same site. Despite his origins, Meadows practised almost exclusively in Devon, remodelling Eggesford House in mid-Devon in 1770–2 and Hartland Abbey in 1779, and it is probably these local connections which persuaded Chichester to employ him.

It was an unfortunate choice. Meadows died at Arlington within a year (he is buried in the church), and the new house was presumably built without his supervision. Contemporary paintings show a plain white-painted building, three storeys high with a bow three bays wide on the south front and canted bays at each end. However, within 30 years it became apparent the house had been carelessly built, and it had to be demolished.

Undaunted, Colonel Chichester hired another architect and began again, this time on a fresh site west of the church. The new man was Thomas Lee (1794–1834) from Barnstaple. He was the son of an

Arlington Court from the east

architect of the same name and was educated at the Grammar School in Barnstaple. For a while in 1810 he was employed in Sir John Soane's office, but left without being articled and entered the office of David Laing, another of Soane's former pupils, then engaged in building the Custom House in Plymouth. He was admitted to the Royal Academy Schools in 1812 and received various awards from the Academy and the Royal Society of Arts. His first major work seems to have been the Wellington Monument on the Blackdown Hills in Somerset, which, except for the projected cast-iron statue of the Duke intended to surmount it, was eventually completed in 1850. (The monument was acquired by the National Trust in 1933.) Ebberley House in north Devon was probably Lee's next work in 1819, followed in 1822 by preliminary designs for Eggesford House in mid-Devon. His other recorded buildings include two churches in Worcestershire and several commissions for Lord Dudley in Staffordshire. His best-known works, however, are the elegant Guildhall in Barnstaple (1826–8) and Arlington Court. He was drowned in 1834 while bathing at Mortehoe near Woolacombe. There is a tablet to his memory on the exterior of the disused chapel of St Anne (now a museum) in Barnstaple.

Although very plain without, Lee's Arlington shows signs of Soane's virtuosity within, particularly the main suite of three south-facing rooms, which, with the Boudoir, remain the best preserved rooms of the 1820s. Elsewhere the house has been considerably altered, most notably by Sir Bruce Chichester in 1864–5. To the north Sir Bruce added a new stone-built wing containing a kitchen, service quarters and bedrooms. The main kitchen now serves as the National Trust restaurant, and a secondary west wing for servants' accommodation has been converted into a modern kitchen and tearoom and offices.

Sir Bruce also added a large dining-room on the north-west side. This later became Miss Chichester's museum and housed many family treasures including a set of four magnificent late eighteenth-century Beauvais tapestries. It must have been a wonderful room. In a dozen or more glass cases or pinned to the wall or standing on the floor or simply 'about the room', as Miss Chichester's own catalogue described them, were exhibits as varied as a lion's claw from South Africa, the Lord's Prayer carved on a cowrie shell, a pair of chief's nose pins from the Solomon Islands, World War I shell cases picked up by Miss Chichester herself on Vimy Ridge, and a 'clay vase from Ur of the Chaldees, 3500 to 3300 BC presented by the excavators in return for pecuniary assistance'. The 1936 catalogue lists over 1,000 items. Tragically, in 1949 the room was found to be riddled with rot and had to be demolished. The tapestries, after a spell at Osterley Park in Middlesex, went to Uppark in Sussex and were eventually rehung at Arlington in 2004.

The stable block

Sir Bruce's other achievement was the stable block and ancillary buildings erected east of the church in 1864 (the date appears in the pediment beneath the clock-tower). It is a fine colonnaded building that bears the Chichesters' heron crest and has housed the National Trust's collection of carriages since 1966 (see p.35).

In 2003 a new carriage museum wing was built on the west side of the courtyard designed by Anthony Harrison.

CHAPTER FOUR

THE PLEASURE GROUNDS AND ESTATE

Arlington Court lies at the centre of a garden and landscaped park within a large agricultural estate, all inherited by the National Trust from Miss Chichester and totalling around 3,500 acres. The estate, which was the traditional means of support for an English country house, comprises rolling hills and valleys straddling the River Yeo on the western fringes of Exmoor, and includes 450 acres of woodland, eight tenanted farms and many cottages in the hamlets of Arlington, Arlington Beccott, Churchill and Loxhore.

A walk to the Stables, about 200 yards due east of the house, provides a first glimpse of several aspects of this inheritance.

THE GARDEN

The garden we see today to the east of the house was largely created in the mid-nineteenth century by Sir Bruce Chichester, and is a modest, but good, example of its kind. The symmetrical design extends across three levels of grass terracing backed by the high kitchen garden wall. On one of the terraces the Trust has re-created circular basket beds filled with colourful annuals, and ironwork frames, up which cobaeas are trained. On the middle level the goldfish pond and fountain are flanked by large Monkey Puzzle trees and arches of common honeysuckle – alternately the Dutch cultivars 'Belgica' and 'Serotina'.

Beyond is the conservatory. This is a replacement, built in 1983 after its Victorian predecessor had rotted beyond repair. A conservatory appears to have stood here for about 150 years, since surviving designs are dated 1849. The new building represents the centre section of its predecessor, which had additional wings on either side (dwarf walls for these can still be seen). The iron heron at the apex of the roof is one of many such birds on estate buildings, which refer to the Chichester crest. The conservatory is planted with such Victorian favourites as agapanthus, plumbago, potted azaleas and lilies.

Behind the conservatory is the walled kitchen garden which is being gradually restored.

Beyond the drive to the south are spectacular clumps of red, pink and white rhododendrons, ferns, pampas grass and gunnera. These hide the Wilderness pond, which was reclaimed from a jungle of undergrowth in the 1970s and at one time sported a black swan. The field above it marks the site of the 1790s mansion, and above that stands an obelisk, erected where a bonfire was lit on 21 June

(Right) The conservatory in the Victorian terraced garden was rebuilt to replace that erected in 1849

The church

1887 to commemorate Queen Victoria's Golden Jubilee. This was a favourite spot for lunch parties, when a tent would be pitched nearby and hot food sent up from the house in hay boxes.

THE CHURCH

From the pond there is a picturesque view of St James's church tower. The church, which does not belong to the National Trust, is well worth visiting. The nave and chancel were rebuilt in 1846 by the Barnstaple architect R. D. Gould, the tower in 1899 (a sketch of the earlier church can be seen in the house).

Inside is a series of monuments to the Chichester family of Arlington: the earliest is Thomasine Ralegh's in the sanctuary; the last, the south aisle monument to Miss Chichester herself, was erected by the National Trust in 1951. This was designed by John Piper and incorporates shells and ferns in reference to her interests. The lettering is by Reynolds Stone.

THE GLEBE HOUSE

The former rectory, now known as the Glebe House and let to a private tenant, stands next to the church. It was built for the Rev. James Chichester, uncle of Sir Bruce, soon after he became Rector of Arlington in 1824, a position he held for 60 years. It is a beautifully proportioned house with double-bowed bays, a shallow slated roof with deep eaves, and a finely curved staircase hall. It was restored in the 1990s.

THE STABLES AND CARRIAGE COLLECTION

The Stables were built in 1864 with spacious loose boxes for Sir Bruce's hunters; they are now used by the National Trust's carriage horses. The remainder of the stable block accommodates an exceptional collection of horse-drawn carriages, which is more fully described in a separate leaflet. The National Trust began acquiring these in 1966, and the collection now comprises nearly 50 vehicles and accompanying harness, some brought from other Trust houses. It includes eight carriages donated by the Marquess of Bute and four bequeathed by Sir Dymoke White. The Science Museum in London has also loaned seven carriages.

The earliest vehicle in the collection is a travelling carriage once owned by the Marquess of Anglesey. It has been conserved by the National Trust, which has pioneered techniques in carriage conservation during the past fifteen years. The finest vehicles are the State Coach from Knole, in Kent, built in 1860, and Lord Craven's State Chariot of 1850. Silver-plated harness from the latter is also on show in the Harness Room.

In 2003 a new purpose-built wing was added to the west side of the yard to provide more space and interpretation for the collection.

(Top) The carriage collection in the new carriage museum

(Above) Lord Craven's State Chariot of 1850

THE GRANARY

The small granary building opposite the Stables entrance was moved here from Dunsland, a fine, mainly seventeenth-century house, which stood 30 miles south-west of Arlington. The National Trust acquired Dunsland in 1954, but it was totally destroyed by a terrible fire in 1967. Photographs and a few relics from the house are displayed inside the granary.

THE AVIARY

West of the house, hidden within a small spinney, is an aviary, home to the peacocks which have been a decorative feature in the Arlington landscape for many years. In the 1920s there were three, known as Spangles, Sapphire and Speckles.

HISTORY OF THE ESTATE

Arlington was already an important land holding by the eleventh century, listed in the Domesday Book as 'Alvered's Manor' and 'Alferdingtonia' and described as an agricultural and wooded estate. By 1700 a landscape of arable fields, meadows and woodland also included large areas of moor and heath. Most of the existing Arlington farmsteads date from this time, although the buildings are mainly later replacements.

In the 1770s the present park was still part of a farmed rather than an ornamental landscape. Enclosures stretched down to the undammed Yeo, the Wilderness was laid out as orchards, and a road ran south from the church and the sixteenth-century manor house to the Yeo east of the Wilderness. By 1800 the landscape had changed considerably: the land had been emparked, but unlike today, the focus of the layout was across East Park (where the obelisk now stands), providing views for Colonel John Chichester's first house of *c.*1790.

The Colonel's son, Sir John, was largely responsible for creating the impressive park landscape as we see it today, both to match the present house, built by his father west of the church, and his own raised status as MP and baronet. By 1842 he had re-oriented the parkland to the west and north to include Middle Park and West Park, while open park also stretched north down into the Yeo Valley. Plantations were laid out on the boundaries of this new parkland: the Brockham Plantation beside the road from Arlington Mill to Brockham Bridge, and another around Town Meadow between the Court and the present car-park. Large plantation nurseries near New England were needed to support this work. Carriage drives were laid out replacing the old road south from the church. The lake, the belts and clumps of trees in the style of 'Capability' Brown, the 'Picturesque' scatter of individual specimens, and the great sweep of grazed parkland were all set within traditional Devon hedge-banks and walls.

The front drive to the north-west of the house was made about 1850 by Sir John. He planned a new entrance from Woolley Lodge on the southern edge of the park on the road to Barnstaple (now the A39). The drive was to plunge down a zig-zag through

Mr Kidwell the gamekeeper, photographed by Miss Chichester

the wood, swoop across the lake over a suspension bridge and thence up through Brockham Plantation to join the present drive to the Court near the Home Farm. A design for the bridge by William Dredge, an engineer, hangs in the Staircase Hall, but at Sir John's death in 1851 only the tall piers had been built and the bridge has remained unfinished.

In the 1860s Sir Bruce Chichester added to the layout by planting the Monkey Puzzle Avenue and the ornamental strip along the northern shore of the lake. He further embellished the landscape to provide a suitable setting for hunting and other traditional Victorian leisure pursuits, but by his death in 1881 the estate was in serious financial difficulty. His widow and daughter attempted to put the farming enterprises on a firmer footing by establishing Home Farm at the end of the century, although unfortunately this entailed subdividing the park.

In later life Miss Chichester had neither the money nor the inclination to keep the estate abreast of modern farming methods. She was more concerned to protect her beloved trees and animals, principally by means of an iron deer-fence, which by the 1930s extended to eight miles. It enclosed a large area of the estate as a deer sanctuary, from which hunting was excluded, and was known as the Reserve. The Trust has respected Miss Chichester's wishes and continues this exclusion, but the deer-fence itself has largely disintegrated. Having no practical role, the unsightly remnants of the fence continue to be removed, although a few short sections, with gates and stiles, are preserved for their historic interest. Arlington's wild red deer are actively protected from poaching and managed by a carefully considered annual cull. The health of the population is the main consideration, with damage to agricultural and forest crops also taken into account.

THE PARK

Arlington's park is of regional importance for its nature conservation interest, particularly for lichens (of which it is the richest site in Devon) and dead-wood invertebrates, notably rare beetles, which thrive on the scatter of ancient trees and associated lying dead wood. Lichens thrive in north Devon's clean air, and the high number of different lichen species at Arlington demonstrates a long continuity of vegetation cover. Open wood pasture must have existed in some form continuously since the Middle Ages to explain this rich diversity of species. In order to promote both dead-wood beetles and lichens, dead and dying trees are being retained where they do not detract from the grandeur of the view from the garden. The Trust has recently restored the treed landscape of the park to its nineteenth-century heyday using the original planting

The memorial urn to Miss Chichester

positions and species, and at the same time is ensuring continuity of habitat by providing new trees for lichens to colonise in the future. Some of the trees are protected by plinth planters – oval raised stone platforms which act as tree guards. New planting includes the restoration of these unusual features. The park is grazed by the descendants of Miss Chichester's flock of Jacob sheep and a small herd of Shetland ponies. Summer grazing by Devon Red cattle has also been introduced for their distinctive traditional appearance and conservation value.

THE LAKE

Arlington Lake was created by Sir John Chichester in 1837 as an ornamental feature by damming the River Yeo and is a rare expanse of freshwater in north Devon. On the north-east shore stands a memorial to Miss Chichester, whose ashes rest beneath it. It was her wish to be buried in this beautiful spot, which is marked by an urn designed by Robert Adam and mounted above an inscription cut by Reynolds Stone.

After Sir John's death in 1851, the lake was extended to its present size. It soon began to silt up, and by the 1930s the upper lake was overgrown with willow. The original island is now lost in the extensive willow carr, ironically part of the Site of Special Scientific Interest (SSSI). The remaining open water continues to cause problems for the Trust. A major dredging project has recently completed the restoration of the lake and dam for the time being, but siltation remains a difficulty.

WILDLIFE

The heron not only features on the Chichester crest, but is also a common sight on the property. A thriving heronry adjoining the lake should be viewed from the hide, as public access is restricted to the area during the breeding season to protect the birds from disturbance. In winter the lake attracts wildfowl, in particular teal, pochard and tufted duck, and all year it is possible to glimpse the turquoise flash of a kingfisher passing by.

A lesser horseshoe bat in flight

Riverside meadows along several miles of the River Yeo form an extensive and interesting wildlife habitat. The conservation of some of these important grasslands is supported by the Countryside Commission's Countryside Stewardship Scheme. Rough grazing here preserves a varied flora and in particular a healthy population of devil's bit scabious, the foodplant of the rare marsh fritillary butterfly. The long continuity of woodland and abundance of large mature trees have created a haven for woodland wildlife such as redstart and pied flycatcher.

The diverse landscape joined by hedgerows and numerous good roost sites make Arlington ideal territory for bats. Pipistrelles and natterer's bats are common, brown long-eared and whiskered bats forage in the woodland, daubentons fly close to the water of the lake, while serotines, lesser horseshoes and noctules are seen over the park. The Court itself has inviting sites for both hibernating and breeding roosts of lesser horseshoe bats. In fact it is the best hibernation site known in Devon, and as an all-year roost is the best in the South West. Part of the basement has been cordoned off and made secure with baffles to enable bats to come and go without disturbance even during the busy visitor season.

WOODLANDS

Records show that Woolley and Deerpark woods are ancient woodlands and as such are highly valuable conservation sites. The area of woodland increased in the nineteenth century, when Scots

The wooded slopes of the Yeo Valley

pine, silver fir and larch were introduced among the oak, beech and Spanish chestnut in mixed plantations. Miss Chichester was reluctant to fell trees, and by the time of her death the woods were becoming overgrown and derelict. In the 1950s and 1960s, active felling and replanting brought new life to the woods, which were then seen primarily as an economic resource for the estate, in line with national forestry policy. Management is now concentrated on eliminating inappropriate species, particularly the invasive *Ponticum* rhododendron planted in the early Victorian period, from the ancient woodlands, where more traditional semi-natural broadleaved trees will be promoted.

FARMS

Although the landscape of the area close to Arlington Court itself has changed considerably over the last 200 years, the surrounding agricultural landscape of the remainder of the estate, and beyond, has remained remarkably stable for centuries. The farms are tenanted and support dairy and stock-rearing enterprises on predominantly rolling pasture land enclosed by typical Devon banks and hedges. In the 1980s many farms were equipped with modern buildings designed to fit the landscape and complement the traditional ones, which are poorly suited to modern agriculture.

ESTATE WALKS

Arlington is a wonderfully tranquil place, and walking its countryside can be rewarding. Although access to the garden, park and lake is restricted to the property's opening times, there are many interesting walks around the estate on public footpaths and permitted routes. A separate countryside leaflet is available which details suggested walks around the park, the plantations to the north-east of the Court towards Arlington Beccott, and a Centenary walk, laid out in 1995 to mark the Trust's centenary year.

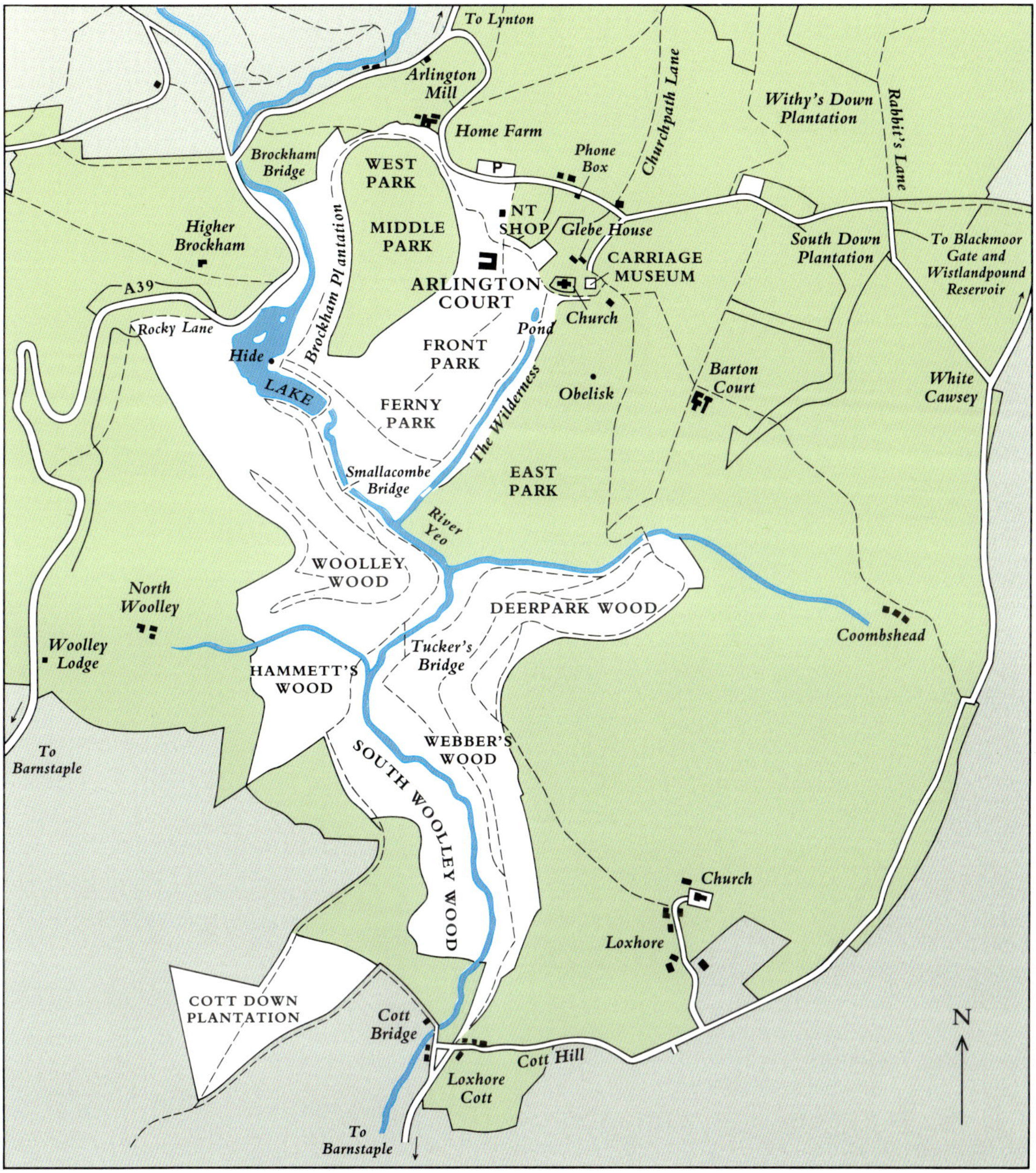

THE ARLINGTON ESTATE

0 ¼ ½ *Scale in miles*

-------- Paths

NT land open to the public

NT land not open to the public

P Car-park

CATALOGUE OF SHIP MODELS

THE ENTRANCE HALL

1 Frigate, 50 guns. A typical example of a French POW bone model mounted on a bone and wooden base. Interesting features include horn wales (the olive green planks below the guns), gold rudder fittings and twin string cords to the stern, which, when pulled, release the guns mounted on a spring mechanism inside the hull. Said to have been made at Millbay Prison in 1810–12.

32 French Frigate, 28 guns. An early nineteenth-century frigate with a characteristically French rounded stern gallery. The model has been re-rigged.

26 Two-decker, 74 guns. The decoration is nicely done with bulkhead screens, driftrails and trailboards on the bow, a Roman figurehead complete with sword, and a slightly over-sized belfry at the break of the forecastle. Most of the rigging is original, with an unusual feature of horn or tortoiseshell stunsail yards rigged on the lower yards.

THE MORNING ROOM

2 *Sovereign of the Seas*, 100 guns. A three-decker built at Chatham and launched in 1637, she was the largest ship of Charles I's reign. One of a pair of models made from brass and bronze, mounted on a bronze sea base and painted gold.

3 HMS *Victory*, 100 guns. Nelson's famous flagship at the Battle of Trafalgar in 1805 was launched at Chatham in 1765 and was a typical three-decker of the mid-eighteenth century. Also in the case is a gun primer from the *Victory*.

4 Frigate. Sailor-made in wood, probably in the early nineteenth century. Shown at anchor in a cove.

5 Sampan. A tortoiseshell model of this Japanese craft, produced in large numbers during the late nineteenth and early twentieth centuries and sold by the local people to seamen and travellers.

6 Ship in Bottle. A typical example of the sailor's craft produced in large numbers and varying styles during the late nineteenth and twentieth centuries. A large ship-rigged merchantman built *c.*1880 probably of steel and of the type used to import nitrates from South America and wool from Australasia.

70 Ship in Bottle. Similar to 6 above, but a two-decker.

THE ANTE ROOM

7 *Gypsy Moth IV*. This silver model of Sir Francis Chichester's yacht was purchased by the National Trust from Garrards to commemorate Miss Chichester's step-nephew's epic round-the-world voyage in 1966–7.

8 Spun and Coloured-glass Ships. A collection probably made in Bristol during the late 19th century.

THE MUSIC ROOM

69 Three-decker. A fine ivory model on an ivory and ebony base.

46 *United LT 192*. A Lowestoft sailing trawler built in 1900 and owned by Orlando F. Mullenden of Lowestoft. She used a beam trawl to catch fish (stowed on deck on the model). In May 1917 she was sunk by a German U-boat. Her waterline is shown on a painted papier-mâché sea base, and she is complete with crew and a helmsman at the wheel.

The three pond model sailing boats on top of the cabinet were sailed by Miss Chichester as a child.

THE STAIRCASE HALL

9 Three-decker, 122 guns. Horn is used for both the main wales and between the guns, probably to illustrate the colour scheme adopted during the early nineteenth century. The silk rigging is mainly original and in good condition. Unusually, the yards are complete with horn stunsail yards.

10 The *Heros*, two-decker, 74 guns. Many POW models were given names of famous French or British ships, whether or not they resembled them. This early nineteenth-century example was probably named after the *Heros*, a third-rate built in 1759 which became a prison ship in 1793.

11 Three-decker, 82–90 guns. Not all bone POW models were rigged, as this hull model mounted on a baseboard illustrates.

12 Frigate, 46–50 guns. A typical example of the 'large frigates' in use during the Napoleonic Wars, with the main armament on a single continuous deck high above the waterline. The fine lines of the hull gave great speed under sail. The full set of anchors is unusual, even though the two at the stern are in the wrong position.

13 Two-decker, 74 guns. A small-scale model of a typical two-decker, which was the mainstay of both the English and French fleets. Probably of box wood, with standing rigging (ie shrouds) made from bone and running rigging from either human hair or more probably a single strand of silk. The sails are cut from wafer-thin shavings of wood and are complete with reefing points. Mounted on an exquisitely decorated and carved hay cart, this is one of the finest French POW models ever made.

14 Brig. The smallest ship in the collection, in a bottle.

15 The *Royal George*, 100 guns. A large first-rate three-decker launched in 1756, she was Admiral Hawke's flagship at the Battle of Quiberon Bay in 1759. She was accidentally sunk at Spithead in 1782 with the loss of 900 lives. The decoration is incorrect: there are too many guns and dolphin strikers and stern davits were not introduced until the late 1790s. This is fairly typical of POW models made in the early nineteenth century.

23 Three-decker, 100 guns. A small-scale model with a bone hull and silk rigging on bone masts and spars. As is common with most POW models, the proportions of the masts and rake of the bowsprit are exaggerated, since the modellers did not have access to scaled plans. The case has small mirrors inside to reflect light into it and show off the hidden side of the model. The exterior has been decorated with plaited and dyed straw, which was easily available to the prisoners, as it was used for bedding.

A bone model of a frigate in the Staircase Hall

16 Four-masted Barque. A sailor-made model, the rig denoted by a fore and aft sail on the jigger mast. The barque is typical of a large merchant ship developed during the late nineteenth century. The lower masts, tops, deck fittings, capstan, boats and decoration are all made of bone, the hull from mahogany.

17 Two-decker, 64 guns. A superb bone POW model with original silk rigging. It portrays a small two-decker with many French features, in particular the shape and layout of the stern galleries. The typically over-scaled but nicely executed figurehead of a Roman warrior is followed by trailboards carved with mermaids. The silk flags include a signal hoist on the mainmast. Between the main and mizzen masts on deck is a compass binnacle with a painted compass inside.

18 Frigate, 46–50 guns. A good and detailed bone model on a marquetry base. It has all the common features: cords to operate the gun mechanism, gold rudder fittings, gold mast hoops, horn upper and lower wales and boats slung from the yardarm tackles and stern davits. The midships or waist screens and bulkheads are decorated with prancing lions and naval trophies.

19 Sloop, 18 guns. An unusual and rare example of POW work where the hull planking is made from strips of tortoiseshell. The sloop was a flush-deck vessel under the command of a lower-ranking officer.

20 Yacht, pond model. Based on the fast cutters of the mid-nineteenth century. Because it is a sailing model, the hull has a deep lead keel for ballast and the basic cutter rig. It was sailed by Miss Chichester's mother when a child.

21 Four-masted Barque. A sailor-made model with mahogany hull and pine sails. The deck planks have been scribed on to wood. Four-masted barques date from the late nineteenth century and had longer mild steel instead of iron hulls, allowing room for the additional jiggermast at the stern.

22 Wooden-screw Sloop, possibly Rosario class. Typical of the fast, heavily armed British screw sloops built in the mid-nineteenth century, which carried a variable armament of guns. The steam-driven screw propeller was hoisted up when under sail and the telescopic funnel was lowered to clear the sails. The model was probably made

up by a sailor or engineer, as the metal fittings are of a particularly high standard.

24 Three-decker, 110 guns. The French were the first to exceed more than 100 guns on a three-decker during the last quarter of the eighteenth century. This particularly fine POW model is unusually detailed, with numerous deck fittings, equipment and beautifully carved officers and men on deck. The silk rigging is mostly original.

THE STAIRCASE

25 *Loch Torridon.* Originally built as a four-masted ship in 1881 for Aitkin, Silburn & Co., Glasgow, she was typical of the big steel vessels of the 1880s. As a colonial trader, her cargoes included grain, wool and nitrates. In 1896 she completed a record-breaking passage from Newcastle, New South Wales, to Valparaiso in 30 days 2 hours. This approximately 1:250 scale model was made by Frank H. Mason in 1925 and depicts her as converted to a four-masted barque after 1912. On 24 January 1915 she was abandoned dismasted in the North Atlantic.

45 *Rose Vine LT 1198.* A Lowestoft steam drifter built in 1913 and owned by George H. Burnwood of Lowestoft. One of many drifters built at the time which soon eclipsed their sailing counterparts, as the 25 hp steam engine produced a speed of 12–15 knots and greatly increased their operational range. The *Rose Vine* was requisitioned in July 1915 and in May 1917 was sunk in a collision off Great Yarmouth. The model depicts the ship drifting with nets being hauled in, close to the South Ower buoy in the English Channel.

28 French three-decker, 110 guns. The red paintwork on the gunport lids is a modern gloss (the original would have been a matt watercolour finish). It has a particularly fine carved figurehead of a Roman warrior with flowing cape.

29 Two-decker, 74 guns. A typical early nineteenth-century bone model. The rigging, masts and spars have been restored. Made with twin pull cords to release the guns and set in a contemporary case with a panoramic background.

30 The *Glory*, 50 guns. A relatively accurate wooden model of a frigate with strips of copper sheeting below the waterline. The exquisite bone figurehead depicts the traditional Roman warrior. The carving in the waist and at the break of the quarter deck are also particularly fine, especially the coat of arms of George I. The guns (turned from brass) include a carronade on the upper deck and conventional cannon on the gun deck. Not comparable with any known ship of this name and date.

31 French two-decker, 74 guns. A rather crudely executed bone model. The over-scaled figurehead, perhaps the head of Mercury, is a replacement. The main and upper wales are of horn, but the hull planking is pinned to a wooden core. The whole model is mounted on a typical bone-covered wooden baseboard.

34 French Frigate, 50 guns. A late nineteenth-century model with rather crude details, which suggests a copy made in the POW style.

35 Two-decker, 90 guns. Comparable to no. 33. A recent gift to Arlington said to have been made, probably in Dieppe, for the Comte de Chambord, the legitimate pretender to the throne of France on the death of Charles X in 1836.

A bone model of a two-decker French frigate stands below a watercolour of Sir Bruce Chichester's topsail schooner 'Erminia'

36 French two-decker, 80 guns. Typically French in showing the ship at anchor on a waterline base. The colour scheme dates from the first quarter of the nineteenth century. There has been some later restoration.

33 Two-decker, 88 guns. The detail and accuracy is exceptional for an ivory model, even down to the numerous carved figures on deck and in the rigging. Remarkably, the sails are made from a single piece of bone, but are nevertheless very realistic. The model has an almost full set of boats, both in the waist and slung from davits. The silk rigging is mostly original.

37 French three-decker, 130 guns. A small-scale, possibly late 19th-century model. The lion figurehead is a later replacement and some of the rigging has been restored.

38 French two-decker, 40 guns. A rather ill-proportioned bone model.

39 *Le Mars*, 74 guns. A typical French model of a two-decker. The painted uniformed figures on the deck and manning the yards are an unusual feature. Probably named after the well-known British two-decker *Mars*, which fought at Trafalgar.

40 Frigate, 30 guns. This rather crude and ill-proportioned model may be a modern replica.

42 *Thermopylae*, Clipper. Built in 1868, she was one of the Aberdeen White Star Line owned by George Thompson & Co., with the distinctive green hull and white lower masts and spars. She completed a momentous maiden voyage to Melbourne in 60 days, beating the record held by the *James Baines* since 1854–5. Her cargoes were mainly wool and tea. She was sold to the Portuguese government in 1896 as a sail-training ship. On 13 October 1907 she was towed out of the Tagus and sunk by gunfire. The approximately 1:250 scale model was made by Frank H. Mason in 1925.

44 *Mizpah LT 607*. A Lowestoft sailing drifter built in 1894 and owned by John Breach of Lowestoft. She was 'dandy'-rigged, ie the mizzen sail is only one-third the size of the mainsail. In 1907 she was lost after a collision with a steam drifter. A sailor-made model, probably by the same hand that built nos. 45 and 46.

THE PORTICO ROOM

43 Two-masted Topsail Schooner. A sailor-made or amateur model of a yacht of similar proportions to Sir Bruce Chichester's schooner *Erminia* (see p.28).

THE SHIP LOBBY

47 HMS *Princess Louisa*. A large-scale model of a two-decker fifth-rate, launched in 1728 and lost in a violent storm off Holland in December 1736. Probably made to hang in church as a memorial to her crew.

41 French three-decker. A good-quality small-scale model in its original straw marquetry and mirrored case. The individual cloths and reef points are marked on the paper sails in pencil or ink. The cords for operating the gun mechanism are led through the middle of the hull at the keel rather than the stern.

27 French three-decker, 100 guns. A small-scale model mounted in its original case decorated with straw marquetry. The bone hull is pierced with brass cannon and retains most of its original rigging. Unusually, the probably silk sails are partially unfurled on the lower yards and fully furled on the upper yards.

48 Three-decker, 96 guns. A bone French model. The rig is slightly ill proportioned, but the hull is well made with decoration carved from single pieces of bone. The boats slung from the yards are probably later replacements, and the rigging has also been extensively repaired. The baseboard is bone with a wooden inlay.

49 Three-masted Clipper. A sailor-made model of a typical clipper very similar in size and layout to the *Cutty Sark* of 1869. Built as fast cargo ships carrying tea, wool or nitrates, the clippers were driven very hard by their masters and owners because early cargoes commanded the best price. She has two small cannons amidships, used for signalling and protection against pirates.

50 Three-decker, 114 guns. Although probably made by a French POW, this wooden model flies British colours to make it more attractive to British buyers. The hull is carved from a single piece of wood, probably box, with intricately carved stern and quarter gallery decoration. Gold is used for mastbands, rudder fittings, lanterns etc.

51 Corvette, 12 guns. A small-scale ivory model. Corvettes carried all their armaments on the upper flush deck and had no quarter deck or forecastle. This model was probably made by the ivory carvers of Dieppe. The hull is typically carved from a solid piece of ivory, together with guns, rigging and sails.

52 Frigate, 50 guns. A relatively accurate model of a French ship, made largely from wood. The hull has individually laid planks glued to a solid core and is finely decorated at bow and stern. The guns have been turned in brass, the rigging is of silk and original.

53 Brig, 10 guns. A relatively common model of an armed brig employed by the French and British navies and in the revenue service. Ivory models like this were probably made in Dieppe. The hull is usually carved from a solid piece of ivory.

54 HMS *Vanguard*, four-decker, 80 guns. Although the name appears on the stern, the model has distinctly French characteristics. The *Vanguard* was, in fact, built in 1787 and used as Nelson's flagship at the Battle of the Nile in 1798. In 1812, she was converted to a prison ship and finally broken up in 1821.

55 Two-decker, 64 guns. Carved from a solid piece of mahogany, this rather simplistic model of a French two-decker is in the style of the later nineteenth-century-made model. The mast tops and anchors are lead.

56 Two-decker, 80 guns. A French POW model made from a variety of materials: box hull, brass cannon, bone deadeyes, waist screens and figurehead and gold on the masts and galleries.

57 Three-decker, 90 guns. The model flies British colours. Horn has been used for the walls, gunport lids and parts of the figurehead. Most of the rigging is original silk. Typically, the longboat is slung from the yardarm tackles between the fore and main masts.

58 HMS *Duke of Kent*, four-decker, 180 guns. An unfinished model of a ship to be constructed at Plymouth in 1809. She was never started. The round bow and stern illustrate a design recently introduced to enable larger and heavier gunned ships to be built.

59 Brig, 12 guns. A very similar model to no. 53.

60 HMS *Trincomalee*, three-decker, 80 guns. A rather crude model of a French three-decker, reputed to have been made in Taunton Prison in 1818. It is carved mainly in wood with a copper bottom. Although there was never a ship of this size with this name, there was a frigate in

Part of Miss Chichester's collection of ship models in the Ship Lobby

1817. The actual vessel survives and is being restored in Hartlepool. She is the second oldest ship still afloat.

61 Two-decker, 74 guns. A French ship and the finest of the wooden models in the collection. The planking on the hull is of box, as is the bow and stern decoration. The guns, both cannon and carronade, are turned from brass and mounted on scale gun carriages. Gold is used on the masts and rudder fittings. The model was originally mounted on a waterline base, but because the hull is so beautifully made it has been raised to be visible. The silk rigging is mostly original. The boats on the base are very detailed: one is a launch with a small carronade on a slide, while others are made in clinker and carvel fashion, all of which have a full set of oars. The figurehead is missing.

62 Frigate, 50 guns. A relatively accurate wooden-hull model of a French frigate, flying British colours. The planking has been fastened to the hull with brass pins which have discoloured the bone, a common problem with these models.

63 *Rising States*, brig, 10 guns. A sailor-made model of an armed brig of the mid-nineteenth century. The hull shape and rig are exaggerated. The name suggests the actual vessel was American.

64 *Annibal*, two-decker, 80 guns. A detailed model of an early nineteenth-century French two-decker. The hull is wooden, sheathed below the waterline in copper. Guns are turned in brass, and gold was used for mast bands and rudder fittings. The name is probably a corruption of *Hannibal*, a two-decker launched in 1786 and captured by the French in 1801.

65 Two-decker, 74 guns. A small scale bone model of a French ship. Most of the rigging is replaced, some in copper wire.

66 Two-decker, 80 guns. A wooden model sheathed below the waterline in a single sheet of copper, secured with brass pins. Gold, silver and lead have been used in some of the fittings.

67 *Gypsy Moth IV*. The ship in which Sir Francis Chichester circumnavigated the globe single-handed in 1966–7. This 1:24 scale model was commissioned by the National Trust from Mr J. R. Varrall.

THE DUNKIRK COLLECTION

These models were specially commissioned by Miss Chichester to illustrate a selection of the varied craft that were employed in the evacuation of Dunkirk, code-named 'Operation Dynamo', on 26 May-3 June 1940. Over 1,300 vessels took part in rescuing over 300,000 British and French soldiers from the beaches of Dunkirk.

In most cases the models, which have been built to varying scales, cannot be identified with a specific vessel, although they are an accurate representation of a class or type that took part in the operation.

D1 Ocean-going salvage tug. Based on the Dutch *Zwarte Zee* which was built in 1933.

D2 Admiralty 'Mersey'-type trawler. Purpose-built at the end of the First World War as a cheap anti-submarine, minesweeping and patrol vessel.

D3 River and estuary tug. Represents the tugs used to tow flotillas of small craft off the beaches at Dunkirk.

D4 Short sea coaster. Very similar to the tramp steamer *Foam Queen*, which returned to Ramsgate on 1 June 1940 with 1,200 men on board.

D5 *Lady of Mann*, Isle of Man steam packet. Built in 1930, she brought back over 4,000 men from Dunkirk and was later involved in the Normandy landings.

D6 Motor picket boat. The standard 45ft Admiralty motor boat, a number of which worked in the shallows picking up men and transporting them to the larger vessels waiting offshore.

D7 Coastal tanker. Took fuel to the expeditionary force.

D8 *Celtic Monarch*, cargo steamer. Delivered supplies to the allied forces.

D9 Steam trawler. Ferried troops and also used for mine-sweeping and anti-submarine patrols. A large number were sunk in action.

D10 Motor fishing vessel. One of the smaller Scottish coastal vessels used at Dunkirk.

D11 Twin-screw motor yacht. One of many small cabin cruisers assembled on the Thames by the Tough Brothers' boatyard. Possibly the *Minnehaha* (now the *Thamesa*), built in 1936. She still survives as a member of the Dunkirk Little Ships Association, formed in 1967.

D12 'R' class destroyer, built *c.*1917. The destroyers were the most important warships involved in 'Operation Dynamo', transporting a third of the troops evacuated.

BIBLIOGRAPHY

PRIMARY SOURCES

Although the family papers relating to the Arlington branch of the Chichester family (deposited in the North Devon Record Office in Barnstaple) are extensive, they contributed little for the purposes of this guidebook. A much more revealing source was provided by Miss Chichester's numerous diaries and photograph albums, which are still kept in the house.

SECONDARY SOURCES

ALDRICH, Megan, ed., *The Craces: Royal Decorators 1768–1899*, London, 1990.

CHICHESTER, Sir Alexander Bruce, *History of the Family of Chichester from AD 1086 to 1870*, London, 1871.

CORNFORTH, John, 'Arlington Court, Devon', *Country Life*, clxix, 30 April 1981, pp. 1178ff.

DRAKE, Sir William, *Notes Genealogical, Historical and Heraldic of the Family of Chichester*, London, 1886.

KINGSLEY, Charles, *Westward Ho!*, London, 1855.

LUMMIS, Trevor, and Jan Marsh, *The Woman's Domain*, London, 1990, pp. 145–67.

LE MESSURIER, Brian, *Arlington Estate* leaflet, Exeter, 1984.

MELLOR, Anne Kostelanetz, *Blake's Human Form Divine*, Berkeley, 1974, pp. 256–70 [on the Arlington Court Picture].

OLIVER, Dr G., *Collection Illustrating the History of Catholic Families in Devon and Cornwall*, London, 1857.

PHELAN, Nancy, *The Swift Foot of Time: An Australian in England 1938–45*, Melbourne, 1983.

ROTHWELL, James, *Thomas Lee, Junior, Architect*, unpublished diploma thesis, Warwick University, 1993.

THOMAS, Graham Stuart, *Gardens of the National Trust*, London, 1979.

TRINICK, Michael, *Arlington Court* guidebook, Plymouth, 1979.

The Staircase Hall; watercolour by Chrissy Peters, c.1914